# THE QUAIL'S TALE

A Story of Survival

in the Sonoran Desert

Written by Natalie Gagnon

Illustrated by Brendon Farley

This book has a Lexile® range of 610-1000L
(Grades 2 to 8)

ISBN: 9781495487750

For Jeff,

who introduced me to the Desert.

# THE QUAIL'S TALE

Winter's gentle rains had passed. The land was alive with new growth. Across the desert, cactuses, plants, and trees were blooming. If a flower was lucky enough to be pollinated, it would become fruit.

Mrs. Quail was restless. She had eggs to lay but didn't know where to lay them. For days, she and her husband had walked about the desert, looking for a suitable place to build their nest. The trees were too high, the cactuses were too prickly, and the rocks were too hard.

Finally, Mrs. Quail walked to a shady area at the base of a smooth, green palo verde tree. She began to scrape the dirt with her feet, using her strong toes to form a shallow bowl in the ground. She gathered a few beakfuls of soft leaves and grasses and placed them into the depression.

"This seems right," she thought as she sat down to rest. Mr. Quail stood off in the distance, watching and waiting. He knew that Mrs. Quail would find the best place for their eggs. It wasn't long before Mrs. Quail laid her first egg into the scrape nest.

Mrs. Quail visited the scrape nest every other day to lay another egg. The eggs were dull white with brown speckles, and no two eggs looked the same.

"Why are you laying your eggs on the ground?" asked the cactus wren. "They will get stepped on by a coyote or stolen by a snake. You should build a dome nest among the sharp spines of a cholla cactus, like me. There, your eggs will be protected."

The Gila woodpecker heard what was going on and joined the cactus wren. "When your eggs hatch," he cautioned Mrs. Quail, "your babies will be out in the open and get eaten by a fox or roadrunner. You should lay your eggs inside a tall saguaro. There, they will be sheltered."

This commotion caught the attention of the white-winged dove, who couldn't resist the chance to offer her opinion. "You are a bad mother," he scolded Mrs. Quail, "laying your eggs among the dirt and rocks. You should make a nest out of twigs in the branches of an acacia tree. There, your eggs will stay warm."

"You are all wrong," chided the burrowing owl, who had popped her head out of her burrow in the desert sand. "You should lay your eggs in an underground burrow, like me. There, your eggs will be hidden."

But Mrs. Quail was not deterred by their suggestions. She believed that her nest was in a very special place. Her eggs blended in so well with their surroundings, they were hidden in plain sight."

"I have always done things in my own special way," she told the birds, "and I see no reason to change now."

When there were 12 eggs in the nest, Mrs. Quail settled down to brood them. Although the eggshells were strong, Mrs. Quail sat lightly on the eggs, warming them with her soft feathers. A few times a day, she rearranged the eggs with her beak so that each egg would be evenly heated.

Mr. Quail was never far from the nest. He watched for danger and waited for Mrs. Quail to join him on their food forages. They preferred to search in the early morning and late afternoon, when the air was cooler and there were fewer predators. Whenever Mrs. Quail left her nest, the other birds would express their disapproval.

"Look at those eggs, sitting there in plain sight," croaked the cactus wren.

"They will not be there for long," added the Gila woodpecker.

Mrs. Quail pretended not to hear them.

Mrs. Quail had been sitting on her eggs for 21 days when she felt some movement. She cocked her head to listen. "Pip, pip, pip," she heard. Then one of the eggs began to crack.

At first, only a small hole was visible, but the little chick inside used its sharp egg tooth to break open a circular "door" in the tip of the shell. "Flip!" opened the door. The chick could be seen breathing inside the shell, its feathers thin and wet.

The tiny chick rested for a moment, then "pop!" out came his head and "foop!" out came his stubby wings. He stopped again, resting his head on the egg next to him. A minute later, the chick gave a great push and "whoop!" out popped his round body and big feet.

The chick sat there for a moment, not quite knowing what to do. Then he got up on those big feet and tried to walk! Mrs. Quail reached down and greeted the chick. "Peep, peep, peep," the chick responded. Soon afterward, the other eggs hatched in the same way. Mr. Quail came by to inspect his new family. He was pleased.

The quail chicks did not look much like their parents, who had mostly grey feathers. The fuzzy chicks were tan with brown stripes, which blended in with their desert surroundings. They had little black feathers on top of their heads, which would grow into fancy topknots like those of their parents.

Their legs were strong and their feet were large, which was a good thing, because they all began to walk minutes after being hatched. At first, they were clumsy, tripping over their own feet, but they soon got the hang of it.

Upon seeing the newly-hatched quail chicks, the other birds had a few things to say.

"My, my, what a shame," the white-winged dove scolded. "Your chicks have hatched and you have nowhere to hide them."

"Yes, they are going to become dinner for a hungry hawk or bobcat," said the burrowing owl.

Mrs. Quail ignored the other birds. She had more important things to look after -- twelve things, to be exact. She was getting hungry, and she knew that her chicks would soon want food as well. "It is time to leave my nest in search of food," she thought. "I must find many leaves, grasses, and seeds to bring back to my chicks." She saw that Mr. Quail was waiting for her to join him.

Mrs. Quail stood up to leave her nest, when something curious happened. Her chicks gathered around her. Mrs. Quail took a step out of the nest. Her chicks hopped out of the nest behind her. Mrs. Quail walked around the nest. Her chicks followed her in a crooked line. "No, you must stay in the nest, where baby birds belong," she warned her chicks. But the chicks stayed right behind her, refusing to return to the nest.

"Those babies are just like their mother," said the white-winged dove; "they don't do what birds are supposed to do."

Mrs. Quail did not answer back. Instead, she looked at her chicks. "Well, if you must follow, you had better keep up," she warned them.

Mr. and Mrs. Quail headed away from the nest, toward the mesquite spring, where they knew they could find food. They were quite surprised that the chicks stayed right behind them. And better yet, they seemed to have no trouble keeping up. These chicks could run!

Now that the chicks were on their feet, the quail family would not return to the scrape nest.

Every day, Mr. and Mrs. Quail took the chicks on outings to find food. Their favorite food was ants, which they ate by the hundreds. Like their parents, the chicks also ate grasses, leaves, flowers, and seeds. If the chicks found a beetle or grasshopper, they feasted! All the water they needed they got from the insects and plants they ate.

Mr. and Mrs. Quail taught their chicks to eat something else that was not food. It was gravel. Small pebbles and bits of sand were swallowed throughout the day. This helped the quails to crush and digest the things they had eaten. (After all, quails do not have teeth to break apart their food, like people do).

As they rested in the shade of a creosote bush, the quail chicks could hear the other chicks in their nests, but they could not see them.

They heard the cactus wren chicks calling from their nest in the cholla cactus. "*Char-char-char*, mother, father, feed us!" they cried.

They heard the Gila woodpecker chicks calling from their saguaro cactus nest. "*Churr-pip-churr*, mother, father, feed us!" they cried.

They heard the white-winged dove chicks calling from their twig nest in the ironwood tree. "*whoo-oo-oo*, mother, father, feed us!" they cried.

They heard the burrowing owl chicks calling from their burrow under the ground "*scree-scree-scree*, mother, father, feed us!" they cried.

The quail chicks said to each other, "Why don't they go out and get their own food, like we do? Can't they take care of themselves? They should try walking instead of crying. What a bunch of babies!"

Mrs. Quail reminded her chicks that it was not nice to make fun of others.

All of this food, exercise, and fresh air was making the quail chicks grow big, healthy, and strong. Every day, they ran faster and jumped higher. It was good they were fast because other creatures in the desert were fast, too - creatures that liked to eat quail chicks.

Instead of fuzzy down, the chicks were now covered with sleek feathers.  Already, they could fly, and they weren't even two weeks old. This was also a good thing, because it meant that they could now roost in the old ironwood tree at night. Each evening at dusk, Mr. Quail flew into the branches of the ironwood tree and gently called his brood, one by one.

"Whit-whit," he called. "Whit-whit," a chick responded. The chick flew into the ironwood tree and Mr. Quail would call the next one. When all 12 chicks were settled with Mr. Quail in the tree, Mrs. Quail joined them. The family nestled together in the leafy, protective branches of the tree, where they were hidden from patrolling owls and coyotes.

One day, the quail family happened upon the other birds. "You are lucky to have so the energy to walk around the desert," moaned the cactus wren. "I am exhausted from building nest after nest after nest in the branches of the chollas."

"Why so many nests?" asked the quail chicks.

"I use them for decoys," the cactus wren responded. "My chicks are all in one nest, but I build many to fool predators."

The Gila woodpecker complained, "You're not the only one who is tired. My neck is stiff from pecking the bark of trees to find insects to feed my hungry nestlings."

Poking her head up from a hole in the ground, the burrowing owl grumbled, "That's nothing. I am worn out from flying around the desert to collect mammal dung for my burrow."

"Why do you do that?" asked the quail chicks.

"The dung attracts beetles to my burrow, which my owlets eat," she answered. "They are still too weak to find food on their own."

The white-winged dove cried, "You think you have problems? My husband and I have flown all the way from Mexico to build a nest and raise our young. We were counting on the saguaro fruit to be ripe, but it's not. Now we have to find seeds for our chicks somewhere else!"

The quail chicks stayed with their parents for twelve weeks. Other quails joined their family group and the covey became a bevy.

In the daytime when the bevy was foraging, one of the quail fathers stood guard atop a cactus or shrub. If he sensed danger, he would give his alarm call, "cre-AR, cre-AR!" and the covey would dart beneath a thicket. Each bird remained perfectly still and oh-so-quiet until the danger passed. If they became frightened, the quail shot into the air all at once in an explosion of fluttering wings and landed a few yards away -- just far enough to escape the danger.

As the chicks grew, summer monsoon rains kept the desert lush. The quail found many plants, fruits, and seeds to eat, along with the occasional insect. Little pools of water formed, where the bevy gathered to drink. Life in the desert was good because it supplied everything the quail needed: food, water, shelter, and space.

By watching their parents, the quail chicks learned many things. They learned which plants to eat and how to behave in quail society. They learned how to be aware of their surroundings and how to avoid predators. Before long, the grown-up chicks were ready to leave the bevy and go out on their own.

One morning, Mr. and Mrs. Quail realized they were once again alone. They foraged during the day and roosted in the ironwood tree at night -- just the two of them. They would try next season to raise another brood.

From time to time, Mr. and Mrs. Quail heard a familiar sound in the distance. It was the sound of one of their grown-up chicks, calling to another quail. Mr. and Mrs. Quail agreed that it had been a successful year because their family went on to live for another generation. They knew that in the springtime, there would be many more restless quails looking for their own special places to lay their eggs.

# ABOUT THE GAMBEL'S QUAIL

The Gambel's quail is named after William Gambel, a 19th century naturalist and explorer of the Southwestern United States. The bird's Latin name, *Callipepla gambelii,* comes from the Greek word *kallipeplos* meaning "beautifully adorned" (from *kalos* meaning "beautiful" and *peplos* meaning "ceremonial robe").  Can you guess where the last part, *gambelii,* comes from?

Both male and female are a blue-gray color with a cream colored belly and a black plume of feathers on the head, called a topknot. Both male and female have rust colored patches on their wings with white streaks. The male has additional markings, including a bright russet cap, a black face with a white border, and a black patch on its belly. Adults are 25 centimeters (9.8 inches) long with a wingspan up to 36 centimeters (14.2 inches). Gambel's quail weigh 160 to 200 grams (5.6 to 7 ounces), with the male slightly larger than the female. Gambel's quail live up to seven years in the wild.

Gambel's quail prefer to walk, but they can fly when escaping danger or to roost in a tree at night. The male and female birds travel in pairs, but in the fall and winter, they form large groups called coveys. Each covey has up to 200 birds!

Gambel's quail have some special vocalizations, or calls. When male and female adult birds want to round up their covey, they call "yhuk-ka-KA!" Whenever a single quail approaches a covey, it nervously calls "whit-whit-whit." When alarmed, the Gambel's quail loudly calls, "creAR-creAR!" to warn the covey of possible danger.

Like many birds, Gambel's quail parents make a good team. Both male and female share in the parenting of their chicks. The female usually incubates the eggs by herself as the male guards the nest. After the chicks hatch, both parents care for the young. If the female is taken away or dies, the male takes over to raise the chicks.

The newly-hatched chicks need protection. As soon as possible, the parents lead their chicks away from the nest. The broken eggshells might make predators hungry for dinner. When danger is near, the quail chicks run to hide under a parent's wing. Young quail do not need care for very long.

They are able to eat food on their own right away. About one week after hatching, they can fly.

After the breeding season, quails form large groups called coveys. A covey can contain as many as 200 birds. Quail in a covey snuggle together when they rest or sleep to keep warm. They search for food together in early morning and late afternoon. They have a better chance of escaping a predator it they stay in a group.

Although quail cannot fly very well, they are very fast runners. When predators come near, quail may run into a thicket where they can escape by staying hidden. Quail that cannot hide will burst into explosive, short-distanced flight to escape danger. Animals that prey on Gambel's quail include snakes, raptors, foxes, bobcats, and coyotes.

# QUAIL VOCABULARY

- A baby quail is a **chick**.

- An adult female quail is a **hen**.

- An adult male quail is a **cock**.

- A group of quail is a **bevy** (large flock) or **covey** (small flock or parents with chicks).

- The plural form of quail is **quail** or **quails**.

- Quails are **diurnal**, which means they are active during the daytime. (From Latin *diurnus* from *diēs* "day").

- Quails are **monogamous**, which means they keep the same breeding mate all their life. (From Greek *monos* "single, alone" and *gamos* "marriage").

- Quails are **oviparous**, which means they lay eggs. (From Latin *ovum* "egg" and *parere* "to bring forth").

- Quails chicks are **precocial**, which means the young are relatively mature and mobile from the moment of birth or hatching. From Latin *prae* "before"and *coquere* "to ripen").

- Quails are **sedentary**, which means they do not migrate. (From Latin *sedēre* "to sit").

- Quails are **social**, which means they live in groups. (From Latin *socius* "companion").

- Quails are **terricolous**, which means they spend most of their time on the ground. (From Latin *terra* "earth" and *colere* "to inhabit").

# Can you spot these Sonoran Desert creatures in the pages of this book?

**American crow**
*(Corvus brachyrhynchos)*
p. 6

**Arizona bark scorpion**
*(Centruroides sculpturatus)*
p. 2

**Arizona desert centipede**
*(Scolopendra heros)*
p. 22

**Armored stink beetle**
*(Eleodes armata)*
pp. iv, 22

**Bobcat**
*(Lynx rufus)*
p. 22

**Cactus longhorn beetle**
*(Moneilema gigas)*
p. 20

# Can you spot these Sonoran Desert creatures in the pages of this book?

**Cactus bug**
(*Chelinidea vittiger*)
p. 20

**California kingsnake**
(*Lampropeltis californiae*)
p. 14

**Collared peccary / javelina**
(*Dicotyles tajacu*)
p. 20

**Cooper's hawk**
(*Astur cooperii*)
p. 12

**Cougar / mountain lion / puma**
(*Puma concolor*)
p. 6

**Coyote**
(*Canis latrans*)
p. 12

# Can you spot these Sonoran Desert creatures in the pages of this book?

**Desert cottontail**
*(Sylvilagus audubonii)*
p. 6

**Desert great horned owl**
*(Bubo virginianus pallescens)*
p. 8

**Glorious beetle**
*(Chrysina gloriosa)*
p. 10

**Gray fox**
*(Urocyo cinereoargenteus)*
p. 24

**Maricopa harvester ant**
*(Pogonomyrmex maricopa)*
pp. 8, 16

**Palo verde beetle**
*(Derobrachus hovorei)*
p. 6

# Can you spot these Sonoran Desert creatures in the pages of this book?

**Sidewinder rattlesnake**
*(Crotalus cerastes)*
p. 12

**Stripe-tailed scorpion**
*(Paravaejovis spinigerus)*
p. 20

**Western desert tarantula /
Arizona blonde tarantula**
*(Aphonopelma chalcodes)*
p. 6

**Western diamondback
rattlesnake**
*(Crotalus atrox)*
p. 26

**Yellow paper wasp**
*(Polistes flavus)*
p. iv

**Zebra-tailed lizard**
*(Callisaurus draconoides)*
p. 4

# PHOTO CREDITS

www.ingramcontent.com/pod-product-compliance
Lightning Source LLC
Chambersburg PA
CBHW041526280526
45792CB00004B/1399